# LANDSCAPES OF THE PASSING STRANGE

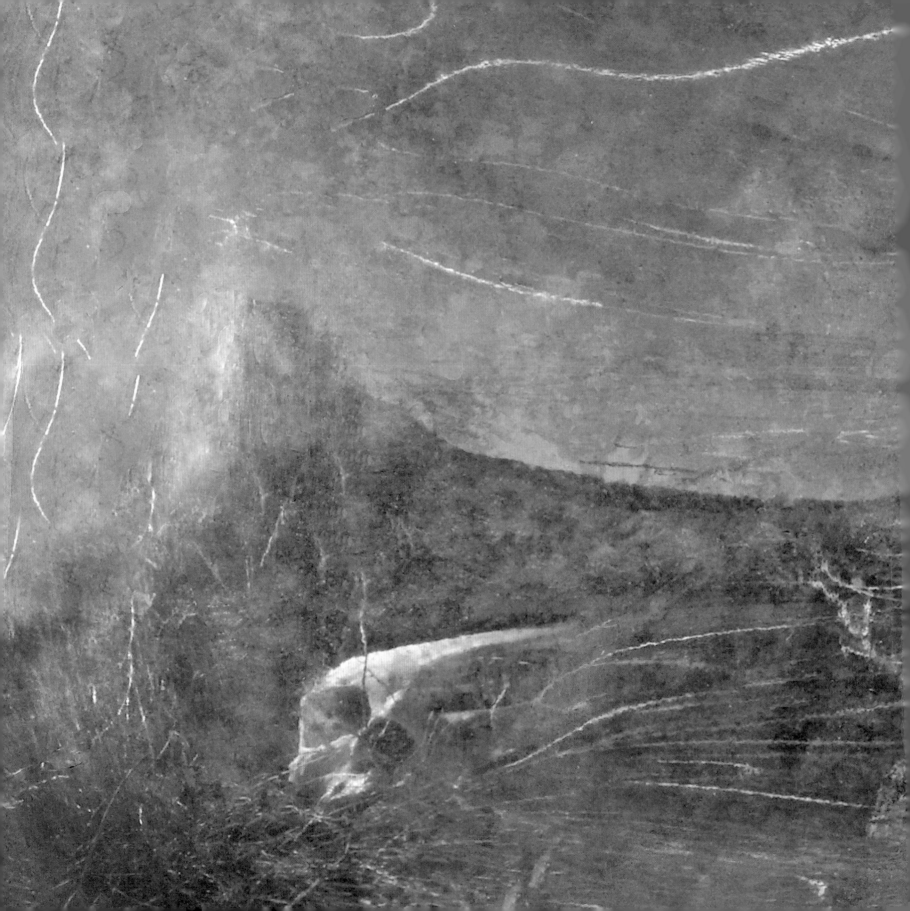

# LANDSCAPES OF THE PASSING STRANGE

## Reflections from Shakespeare

ROSAMOND PURCELL AND MICHAEL WITMORE

W. W. Norton & Company

New York * London

*With love to my siblings: Jamie, Robby, and Katy Wolff* —RWP

*To Kellie, who sees* —MW

TITLE PAGE: *The Undiscovered Country*

Copyright © 2011 by Rosamond Purcell and Michael Witmore

All quotations from Shakespeare are taken from *The Norton Shakespeare,* Second Edition, Stephen Greenblatt, Walter Cohen, Jean E. Howard, and Katharine Eisaman Maus, eds. (New York: W. W. Norton & Company, 2008). References to *King Lear* are to the 1623 Folio version, which Norton prints separately as *The Tragedy of King Lear.* In the rare case where material has been omitted from a quoted passage, that omission is indicated with an ellipsis. Where a quoted passage begins or ends mid-sentence, we have chosen in general not to indicate sentence boundaries with opening and closing ellipses.

For information about permission to reproduce selections from this book, write to
Permissions, W. W. Norton & Company, Inc., 500 Fifth Avenue, New York, NY 10110

For information about special discounts for bulk purchases, please contact
W. W. Norton Special Sales at specialsales@wwnorton.com or 800-233-4830

Manufacturing by Mondadori, Verona, Italy

Book design and composition by Laura Lindgren

Library of Congress Cataloging-in-Publication Data
Purcell, Rosamond Wolff.
  Landscapes of the passing strange : reflections from Shakespeare / Rosamond Purcell and Michael Witmore. — 1st ed.
    p. cm.
  ISBN 978-0-393-33948-2 (pbk.)
  1. Shakespeare, William, 1564–1616—Illustrations.  I. Witmore, Michael. II. Title.
  PR2883.P87 2010
  822.3'3—dc22    2010018277

W. W. Norton & Company, Inc., 500 Fifth Avenue, New York, N.Y. 10110 | www.wwnorton.com

W. W. Norton & Company Ltd., Castle House, 75/76 Wells Street, London W1T 3QT

1 2 3 4 5 6 7 8 9 0

# CONTENTS

## MADLY SHOT STARS

Once I sat upon a promontory
And heard a mermaid on a dolphin's back
Uttering such dulcet and harmonious breath
That the rude sea grew civil at her song
And certain stars shot madly from their spheres
To hear the sea-maid's music.

—Oberon, *A Midsummer Night's Dream*, 2.1

# MORE STRANGE THAN TRUE

## Michael Witmore

Shakespeare thought in pictures. Consider this set of images, taken from *Romeo and Juliet*, used to describe a tiny chariot driven by Queen Mab, the midwife of the fairies:

> Her wagon spokes made of long spinners' legs;
> The cover, of the wings of grasshoppers;
> Her traces [harness], of the moonshine's wat'ry beams;
> Her collars, of the smallest spider web;
> Her whip, of cricket's bone, the lash of film.  (1.4.60–64)

This is only a small fragment of a much longer portrait, but even in five lines we hear the mental shutter clicking furiously away. Spinners' legs and wagon spokes: click. Grasshopper wings, iridescent as the halo of the moon: click. Harnesses and collars linked by a fine spun web or liquid filaments of light: click.

There is a magic in words that make a whip handle of a cricket's bone. A similar magic takes place in photography, which is why it seems appropriate to pair the words of Shakespeare's plays with images from the camera. Such pairings speak for themselves: they require no introduction here. But it is worth thinking briefly about how Shakespeare's words work, since they lend themselves so readily to the metamorphoses that take place within the picture frame. What is it about Shakespeare's language that makes this type of pairing possible or interesting? What, before the shutter snaps, is already lying there in the lines, waiting to be seen?

It is hard sometimes simply to understand what Shakespeare's words mean. Images grow in tangles, like the riotous buds of green and white that spiral through the foreground of the photograph below.

*An Art That Nature Makes*

Coleridge once described Shakespeare as "myriad-minded," a phrase that suggests the playwright's mind multiplied ideas by the thousands. Perhaps it was Shakespeare's penchant for thinking in pictures that encouraged this vernal surge of associations—what the earth goddess Ceres in *The Tempest* calls "foison plenty."

But verbal images like that of Queen Mab's wagon have a practical function, providing what we might call a "script within the script," a way of approaching the action or ideas that are unfolding onstage. Shakespeare made use of this *second* script of images for obvious reasons: working in a theatrical medium that relied primarily on physical bodies and voices, he did not have access to the cinematic flashbacks, digital animation, and luxurious soundtrack that storytellers employ today. Rather, he used imagery—lots and lots of it—to suggest how an actor or audience member should feel about a particular moment in the story.

The results of this technique are visually and aurally arresting, pointing us toward what literal sight cannot convey. A beautiful illustration of this process appears in *Antony and Cleopatra*, at the moment Antony realizes he has lost a decisive battle to Caesar.

ANTONY: The hearts
That spanieled me at heels, to whom I gave
Their wishes, do discandy, melt their sweets
On blossoming Caesar. (*Antony and Cleopatra*, 4.13.20–23)

The words here compose a surreal scene, like a Salvador Dalí painting with its melting clocks. Antony's friends have abandoned him and taken up with his enemy: this shift in allegiance is compared to a dog who begs a piece of candy under the table (at heels) and then dissolves the sugary coating of these sweetmeats on a new master who grows like a flower. It is an odd set of images, but it *shows* something in a way that simply reporting the action cannot: the fickleness of Antony's allies—who are only too eager to trade love for attention—and the impermanence of favors (sweets) that seem to dissolve as soon as the giver is gone. From hearts to spaniels to heels; from wishes to candy to blossoms: Shakespeare's images move as quickly as an eye across a landscape or a crowded room.

That crowded room was often a theater, and Shakespeare needed to find ways of gesturing beyond the walls of the "wooden O" where his plays were performed. His audience would have enjoyed hearing Oberon, the king of the fairies, tell his servant Puck to fetch an herb and return before "the leviathan can swim a league" (*A Midsummer Night's Dream*, 2.1.174). How much better, when trying to imagine an interval of time, to think about a sea monster surging through the deep than an hourglass dropping sand?

*Leviathan*

Most critics agree that the plays were written to be performed rather than read, but the presence of such images rewards close attention and patient reading. Regardless of how we approach this second, imagistic script in Shakespeare, it stands as a window through which to glimpse whatever it was that he and his company wanted to produce in the mind's eye. His language directs us to that other place where theatrical events happen: not on the stage but in the shuttered world of the imagination.

*

Clearly the mind contributes something to vision, a contribution that cognitive scientists now investigate with the elaborate machinery of magnetic resonance imaging. Something similar can be shown with Shakespeare's words, which are themselves a record of the mind's traffic with images. In the Shakespearean darkroom, we regularly see pictures forming—for example, that of the wagon pulled by threads of moonbeam—that are more than optical records of phenomena in the world.

As Shakespeare writes in one of his sonnets, the outward eye that transmits sensations to the soul can be overwhelmed by an inner one: "Since I left you mine eye is in my mind," he writes in the first line, suggesting that this inner, mind's eye works opportunistically, bringing to thought what the speaker most wants to see.

> The mountain or the sea, the day or night,
> The crow or dove, it shapes them to your feature.
> Incapable of more, replete with you,
> My most true mind thus makes mine eye untrue. (Sonnet 113, 11–14)

We see, then, what we love, desire, and fear. Equipped with its own image-making faculty—what in the Renaissance was called "phantasy" or "fancy"—the soul entertains a variety of images, some of which are accurate impressions of sensation, others confections of memory or imagination. Four hundred years later, we have very different technologies for understanding the mind and for capturing images. But we still believe that the mind sees more than what the eyes convey.

Shakespeare comments on this phenomenon frequently. When Hamlet and Polonius are looking at clouds in the sky, the prince sees a menagerie.

> HAMLET: Do you see yonder cloud that's almost in shape of a camel?
> POLONIUS: By th' mass, and 'tis: like a camel, indeed.
> HAMLET: Methinks it is like a weasel.

POLONIUS: It is backed like a weasel.

HAMLET: Or like a whale.

POLONIUS: Very like a whale. (*Hamlet*, 3.2.345–351)

Polonius is easily led, and in any event he is in no mood to cross the prince. The images here—camel, weasel, whale—suggest a pictorial mind in motion, either the hero's or the playwright's. Duke Theseus identifies a similar receptiveness to forms in *A Midsummer Night's Dream* when he sums up the fantastic events occurring in the forest of Athens. "More strange than true," he begins, concluding that "strong imagination" has led the lovers to see things that simply could not be. In the night, he says, "imagining some fear, / How easy is a bush supposed a bear" (5.1.2, 21–22).

Such mistakes may be ridiculous, but nevertheless they demonstrate the capacity of the eye to be guided by words. The lover, poet, and madman are all taken with such "shaping fantasies" (5.1.5), Theseus says, but clearly they are not the only ones. We do not have to be delirious to see and hear things in the woods of Shakespeare's language, things that connect with our own history, hopes, and fears. Pictures can capture these connections, drawing an arboreal canopy of emotion across the landscape, shadowing it in mood. As anyone who has read a Shakespeare play knows already, not all of these emotions and moods are playful. There are terrors in these plays: think of the vast, god-emptied skies in *Lear*, of Henry V's decision to massacre his French prisoners, or the rudderless drift of Ophelia's songs. Nature makes no promise that the worst will be avoided.

There are also moments of impossibly delicate hope, moments that can be apprehended only glancingly in a world aware of its own failings. "It is required you do awake your faith," Paulina says in *The Winter's Tale*, preparing to bring a statue of the long-dead Hermione to life. In this story about the consequences of jealousy, Shakespeare revives the abandoned hopes of his characters with a coup de theatre: the woman who was killed by her husband's accusations of adultery will be revived before his very eyes. What does such an impossible revival, of persons and of hopes, look like? It is something one might wish to capture in a picture.

Music strikes, the hand reaches out expectantly.

Somewhere a swan is singing.

In the glassy distance, another life appears.

THE MESSENGER APPROACHES

When the oracle...
Shall the contents discover, something rare
Even then will rush to knowledge.

—Dion, *The Winter's Tale*, 3.1

FALSTAFF'S ESCAPE

Look, here is a basket. If he be of any reasonable stature, he may creep in here;
and throw foul linen upon him as if it were going to bucking.

—Mistress Page, *The Merry Wives of Windsor*, 3.3

## AN ART THAT NATURE MAKES

Over that art
Which you say adds to nature is an art
That nature makes.

—Polixenes, *The Winter's Tale*, 4.4

MALAPROP CONSTABLE

O villain! Thou wilt be condemned into everlasting redemption for this.

—Dogberry, *Much Ado About Nothing*, 4.2

### RUDE MECHANICALS

While she was in her dull and sleeping hour
A crew of patches, rude mechanicals
That work for bread upon Athenian stalls,
Were met together to rehearse a play.

—Robin, *A Midsummer Night's Dream*, 3.2

### THE BLASTED HEATH

Say from whence
You owe this strange intelligence, or why
Upon this blasted heath you stop our way
With such prophetic greeting.

—Macbeth, *Macbeth*, 1.3

AWAKE YOUR FAITH

If you can behold it,
I'll make the statue move indeed, descend,
And take you by the hand.

—Paulina, *The Winter's Tale*, 5.3

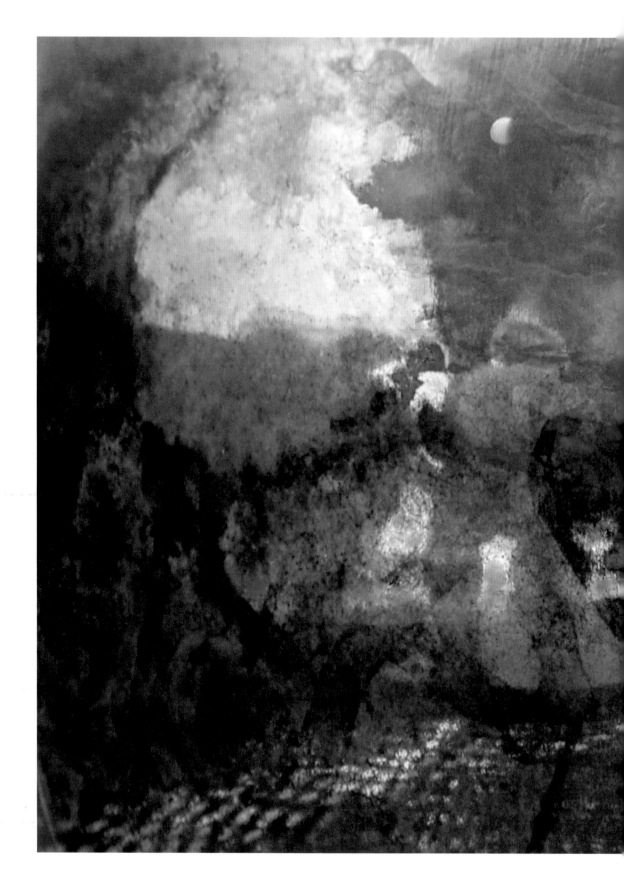

## THE OSTLER'S PLACE

Heigh-ho! An't be not four
by the day, I'll be hanged.
Charles's Wain is over the new
chimney, and yet our horse
not packed. What, ostler!

—First Carrier, *1 Henry IV*, 2.1

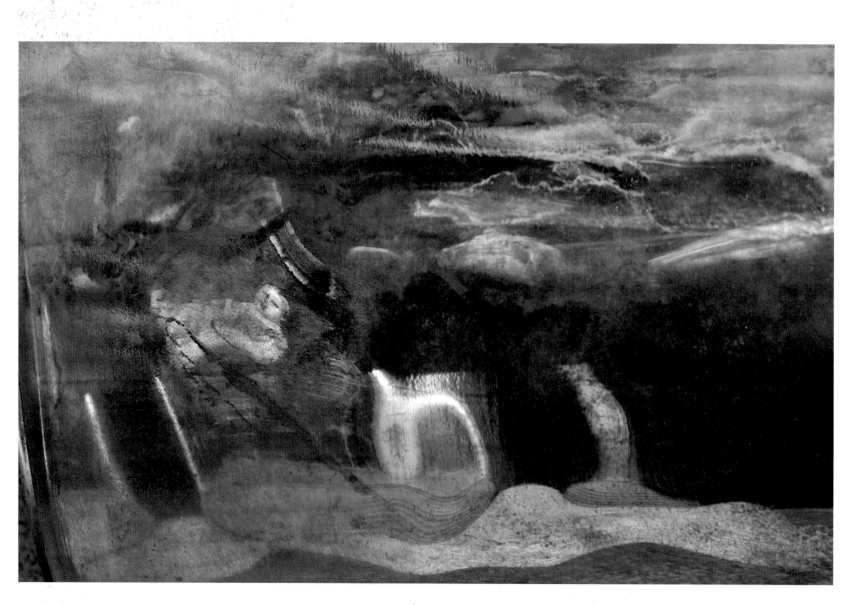

PERDITA'S LANDING

Poor wretch,
That for thy mother's fault art thus exposed
To loss and what may follow!

—Antigonus, *The Winter's Tale*, 3.3

## OPEN YOUR EARS

Open your ears; for which of you will stop
The vent of hearing when loud Rumour speaks?

—Rumour, *2 Henry IV*, Induction

## REMEMBERING OLD ST. PAUL'S

I bought him in Paul's, and he'll buy me a horse in Smithfield. An I could get me but a wife in the stews, I were manned, horsed, and wived.

—Falstaff, *2 Henry IV*, 1.2

ALL ARE FLED

Tom will make him weep and wail;
For with throwing thus my head,
Dogs leapt the hatch, and all are fled.

—Edgar, *King Lear*, 3.6

### LIE FURTHER OFF

But, gentle friend, for love and courtesy,
Lie further off, in humane modesty.

—Hermia, *A Midsummer Night's Dream*, 2.2

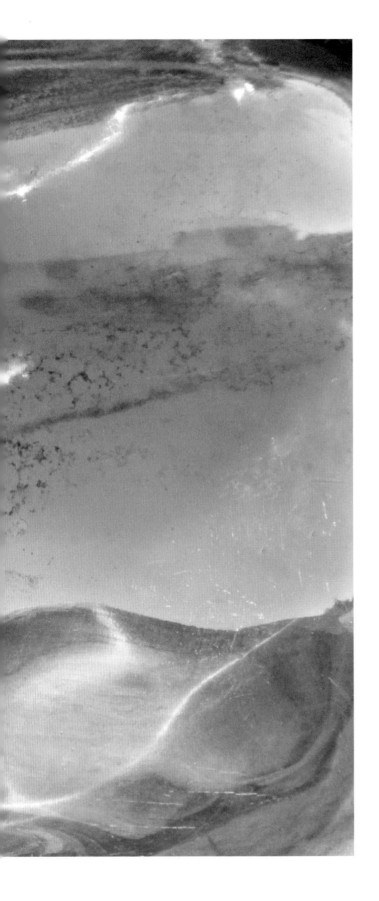

## REMEMBER ME

Upon my secure hour thy uncle stole
With juice of cursèd hebenon in a vial,
And in the porches of mine ears did pour
The leperous distilment.

—Ghost, *Hamlet*, 1.5

OTHELLO GREETS DESDEMONA IN CYPRUS

O my fair warrior!

—Othello, *Othello*, 2.1

## BORING THE MOON

O, the most piteous cry of the poor souls!
Sometimes to see 'em, and not to see 'em;
now the ship boring the moon
with her mainmast, and anon
swallowed with yeast and froth,
as you'd thrust a cork into a hogshead.

—Clown, *The Winter's Tale*, 3.3

## TWENTY SHADOWS

Each substance of a grief hath twenty shadows
Which shows like grief itself but is not so.
For sorrow's eye, glazèd with blinding tears,
Divides one thing entire to many objects—
Like perspectives, which, rightly gazed upon,
Show nothing but confusion; eyed awry,
Distinguish form.

—Bushy, *Richard II*, 2.2

### THE RETURN TO ELSINORE

Ere we were two days old at sea,
a pirate of very warlike appointment gave us chase...
in the grapple I boarded them.

—Hamlet, *Hamlet*, 4.6

## MIRANDA SEES THE STORM

If by your art, my dearest father, you have
Put the wild waters in this roar, allay them.
The sky, it seems, would pour down
        stinking pitch,
But that the sea, mounting to th'
        welkin's cheek,
Dashes the fire out. O, I have sufferèd
With those that I saw suffer!

—Miranda, *The Tempest,* 1.2

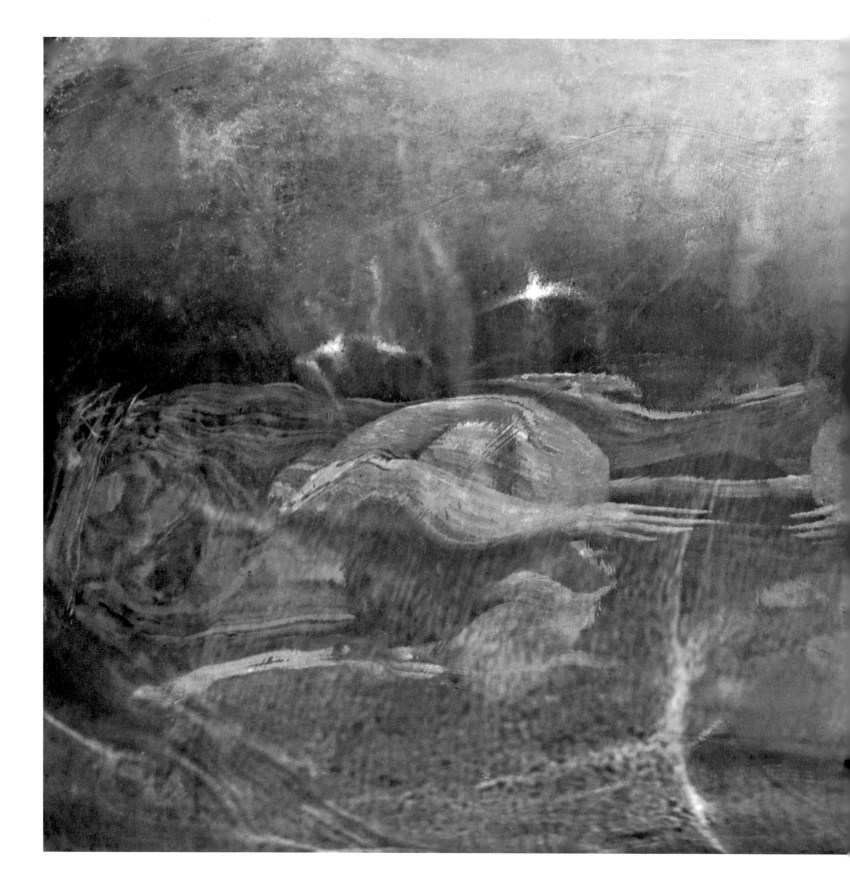

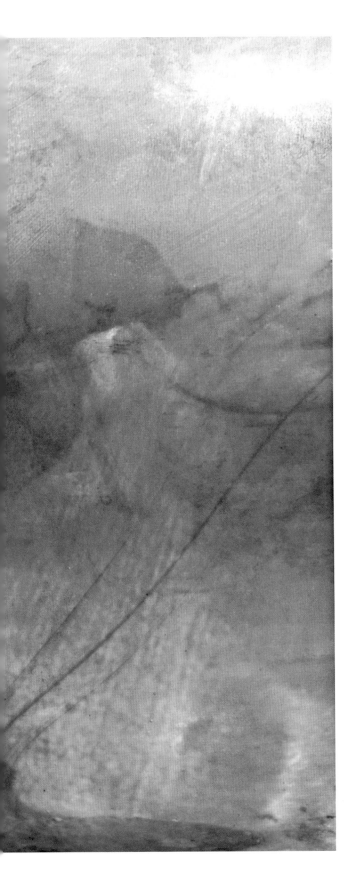

CALIBAN'S FREEDOM

'Ban, 'ban, Cacaliban
Has a new master.—Get a new man!

—Caliban, *The Tempest*, 2.2

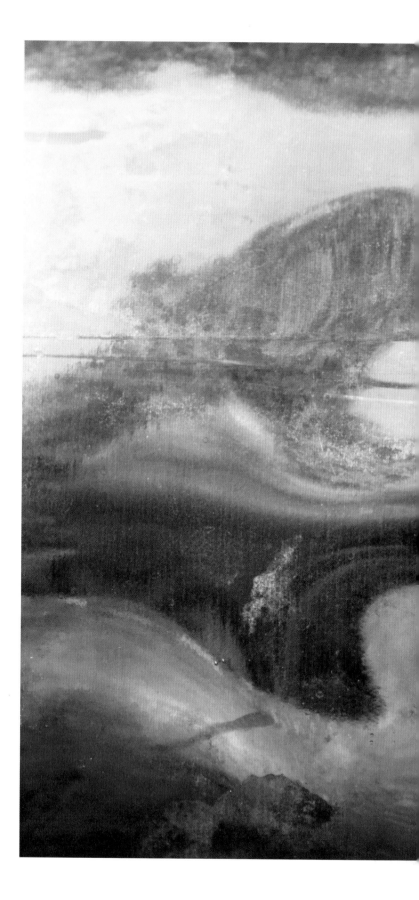

## TO ONE THING CONSTANT NEVER

Sigh no more, ladies, sigh no more.
Men were deceivers ever,
One foot in sea, and one on shore,
To one thing constant never.

—Balthasar, *Much Ado About Nothing*, 2.3

### GREY-EYED MORN

The grey-eyed morn smiles on the frowning night,
Chequ'ring the eastern clouds with streaks of light,
And fleckled darkness like a drunkard reels
From forth day's path and Titan's fiery wheels.

—Friar Laurence, *Romeo and Juliet*, 2.2

### FERDINAND HEARS ARIEL'S SONG

Where should this music be? I'th' air or th'earth?…
This is no mortal business, nor no sound / That the earth owes.

—Ferdinand, *The Tempest*, 1.2

DESCANT ON MY DEFORMITY

I that am curtailed of this fair proportion,
Cheated of feature by dissembling nature,
Deformed, unfinished, sent before my time
Into this breathing world.

—Richard, Duke of Gloucester, *Richard III*, 1.1

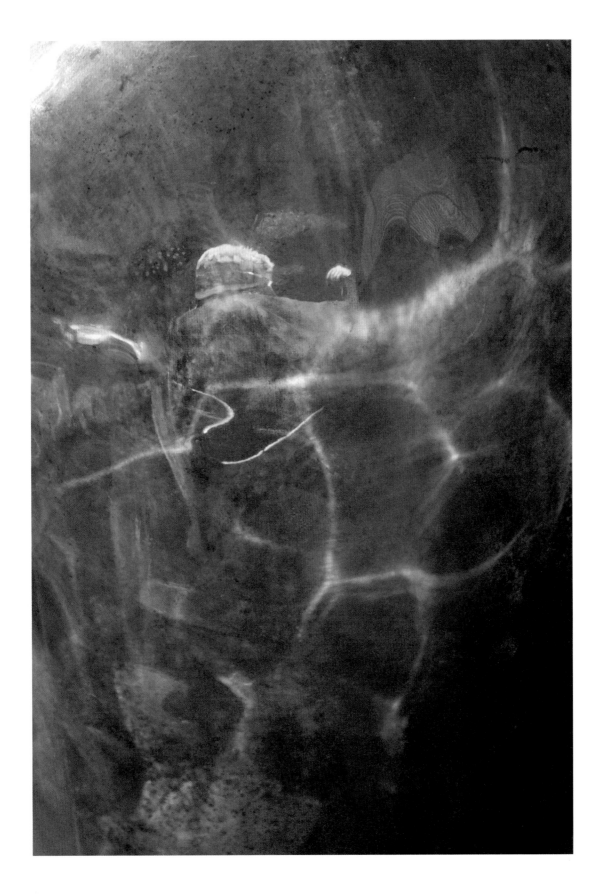

### AUMERLE SPEEDS TO THE KING

After, Aumerle! Mount thee upon his horse.
Spur, post, and get before him to the King,
And beg thy pardon ere he do accuse thee.
...Away, be gone!

—Duchess of York, *Richard II*, 5.2

### BARREN WINTER

Thus sometimes hath the brightest day a cloud;
And after summer evermore succeeds
Barren winter, with his wrathful nipping cold;
So cares and joys abound as seasons fleet.

—Duke Humphrey of Gloucester, *2 Henry VI*, 2.4

## THE WARS TO COME

And in this seat of peace tumultuous wars
Shall kin with kin and kind with kind confound.
Disorder, horror, fear, and mutiny
Shall here inhabit, and this land be called
The field of Golgotha and dead men's skulls.

—Bishop of Carlisle, *Richard II*, 4.1

## MASSACRE

But hark, what new alarum is this same?
The French have reinforced their scattered men.
Then every soldier kill his prisoners.
Give the word through.

—King Harry, *Henry V*, 4.6

FEEDING ON ENGLAND

By devilish policy art thou grown great,
And like ambitious Sylla, overgorged
With gobbets of thy mother's bleeding heart.

—Captain, *2 Henry VI*, 4.1

## THE FIELD OF CLOTH OF GOLD

Today the French,
All clinquant all in gold, like heathen gods
Shone down the English; and tomorrow they
Made Britain India.

—Norfolk, *All Is True* (*Henry VIII*), 1.1

## IN SPRINGTIME

And therefore take the present time,
　　With a hey, and a ho, and a hey-nonny-no,
For love is crownèd with the prime,
　　In spring time, the only pretty ring-time.

—Pages, *As You Like It*, 5.3

### KISSING-COMFITS

Let the sky rain potatoes, let it thunder to the tune of "Greensleeves,"
hail kissing-comfits, and snow eringoes.

—Falstaff, *The Merry Wives of Windsor*, 5.5

## AN EMPTY SET

All the world's a stage,
And all the men and women merely players.

—Jaques, *As You Like It*, 2.7

THE COWARDLY EARTH

At my nativity
The front of heaven was full of fiery shapes,
Of burning cressets; and at my birth
The frame and huge foundation of the earth
Shaked like a coward.

—Glyndŵr, *1 Henry IV*, 3.1

YOUTH IN WINTER

Pardon, old father, my mistaking eyes
That have been so bedazzled with the sun
That everything I look on seemeth green.

—Katherine, *The Taming of the Shrew*, 4.6

## DEAF AND DULL

The woods are ruthless, dreadful, deaf, and dull.
There speak and strike, brave boys, and take
your turns.
There serve your lust,
shadowed from heaven's eye,
And revel in Lavinia's treasury.

—Aaron, *Titus Andronicus*, 2.1

THE CONJURER, PROSPERO

Come away, servant, come! I am ready now.
Approach, my Ariel, come!

—Prospero, *The Tempest*, 1.2

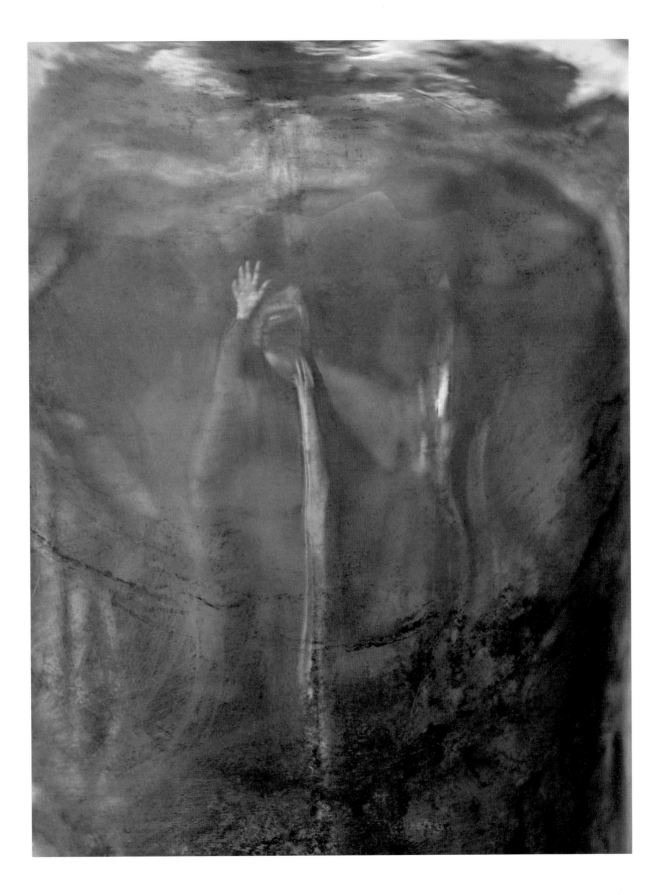

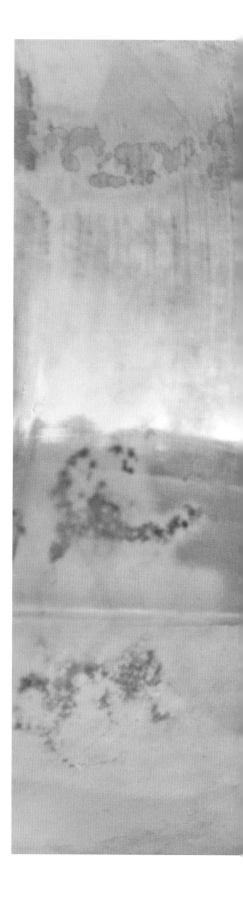

A DUCHESS'S CURSE

Dead life, blind sight, poor mortal living ghost,
Woe's scene, world's shame, grave's due by life usurped...
Rest thy unrest on England's lawful earth,
Unlawfully made drunk with innocents' blood.

—Duchess of York, *Richard III*, 4.4

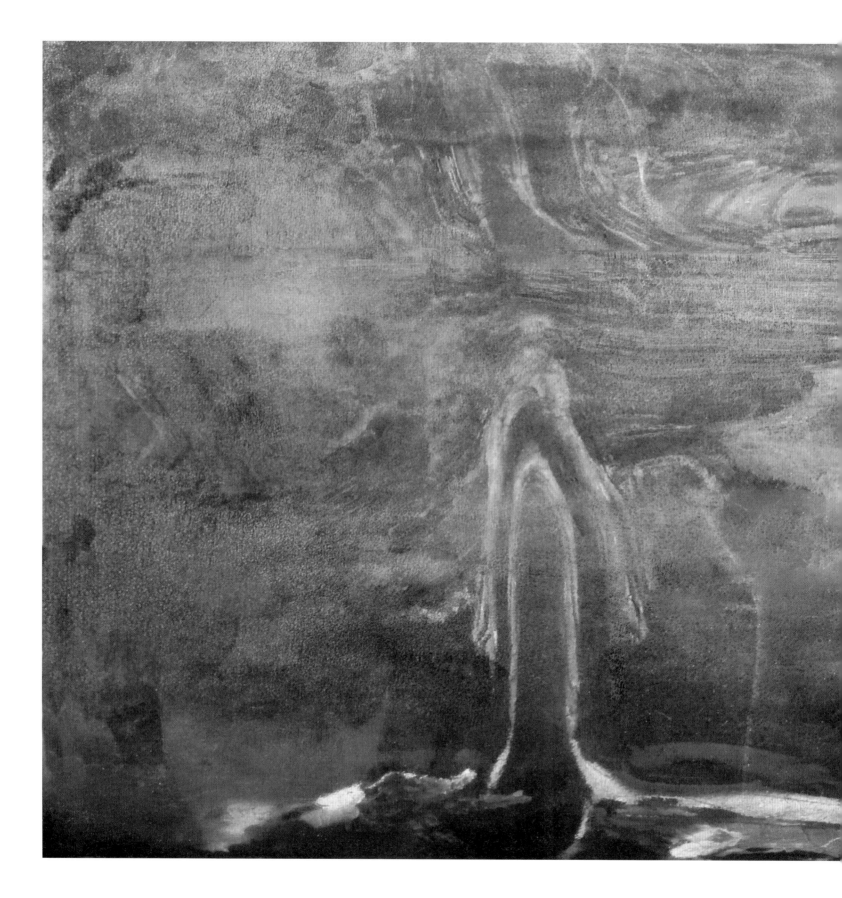

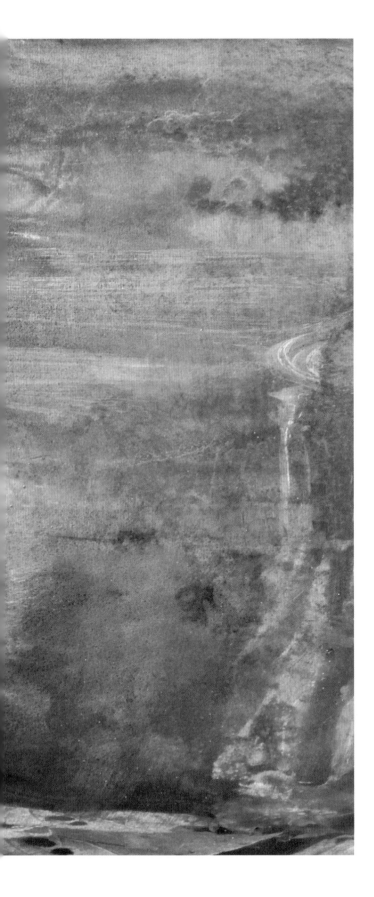

BARE FORKED ANIMAL

Thou art the thing itself. Unaccommodated man is no more but such a poor, bare, forked animal as thou art.

—Lear, *King Lear*, 3.4

## THE PREPARATION OF OPHELIA

Is she to be buried in Christian burial
that wilfully seeks her own salvation?

—First Clown, *Hamlet*, 5.1

## DREAMERS OFTEN LIE

I dreamt a dream tonight.

—Romeo, *Romeo and Juliet*, 1.4

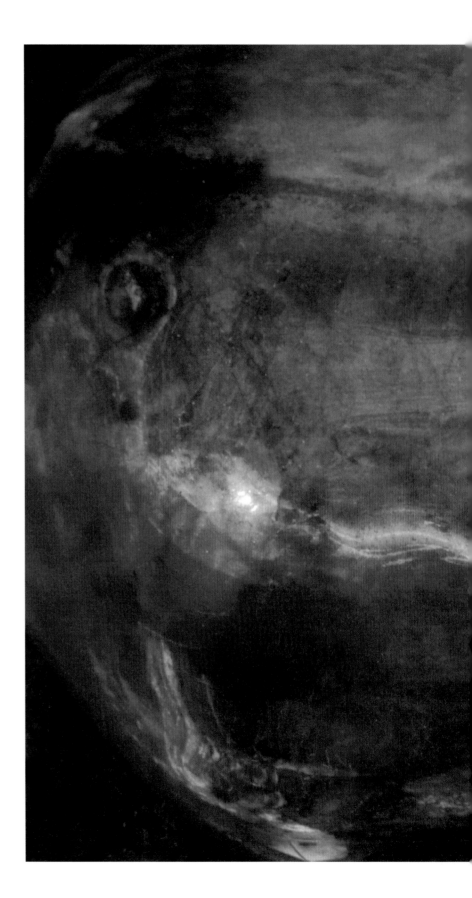

THE SWELLING SCENE

O for a muse of fire, that would ascend
The brightest heaven of invention:
A kingdom for a stage, princes to act,
And monarchs to behold the swelling scene.

—Chorus, *Henry V*, Prologue

### THE PENALTY

The pound of flesh which I demand of him
Is dearly bought. 'Tis mine, and I will have it.

—Shylock, *The Merchant of Venice*, 4.1

'TIS THE EYE OF CHILDHOOD
Give me the daggers. The sleeping and the dead
Are but as pictures. 'Tis the eye of childhood
That fears a painted devil.

—Lady Macbeth, *Macbeth*, 2.2

## UNBURIED

Titus unkind, and careless of thine own,
Why suffer'st thou thy sons unburied yet
To hover on the dreadful shore of Styx?

—Titus, *Titus Andronicus*, 1.1

THE BOOK, THE LAND

In nature's infinite book of secrecy
A little I can read.

—Soothsayer, *Antony and Cleopatra*, 1.2

## SUBTLE AS SPHINX

Subtle as Sphinx, as sweet and musical
As bright Apollo's lute strung with his hair;
And when love speaks, the voice of all the gods
Make heaven drowsy with the harmony.

—Biron, *Love's Labour's Lost*, 4.3

THIS QUEEN WILL LIVE

This queen will live. Nature awakes, a warmth
Breathes out of her. She hath not been entranced
Above five hours. See how she 'gins to blow
Into life's flow'r again.

—Cerimon, *Pericles*, Scene 12

LET HELEN GO

Cry, Trojans, cry! Ah Helen, and ah woe!
Cry, cry "Troy burns!"—or else let Helen go.

—Cassandra, *Troilus and Cressida*, 2.2

## HEAVEN'S VAULT

Howl, howl, howl, howl! O, you are men of stones.
Had I your tongues and eyes, I'd use them so
That heaven's vault should crack. She's gone for ever.
I know when one is dead and when one lives.
She's dead as earth.

—Lear, *King Lear*, 5.3

## WE ARE PICTURES

Poor Ophelia
Divided from herself and her fair judgement,
Without the which we are pictures or mere beasts.

—Claudius, *Hamlet*, 4.5

PETRUCCIO'S HORSE

Full of windgalls, sped with spavins, rayed with the yellows, past cure of the fives,
stark spoiled with the staggers, begnawn with the bots,
weighed in the back and shoulder-shotten,
near-legged before and with a half-cheeked bit....

—Biondello, *The Taming of the Shrew*, 3.2

### TILL THAT HER GARMENTS

Till that her garments, heavy with their drink,
Pulled the poor wretch from her melodious lay
To muddy death.

—Gertrude, *Hamlet*, 4.7

### THE SOUNDS AT DOVER CLIFFS

There is a cliff whose high and bending head
Looks fearfully in the confinèd deep.
Bring me but to the very brim of it.

—Gloucester, *King Lear*, 4.1

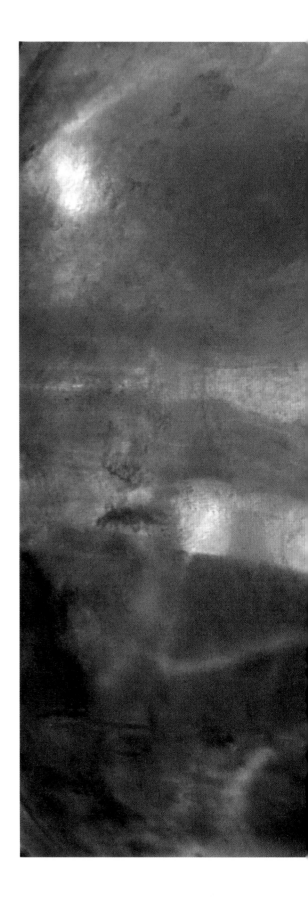

### KNOW MY STOPS

You would play upon me, you would seem to know my stops,
you would pluck out the heart of my mystery.

—Hamlet, *Hamlet*, 3.2

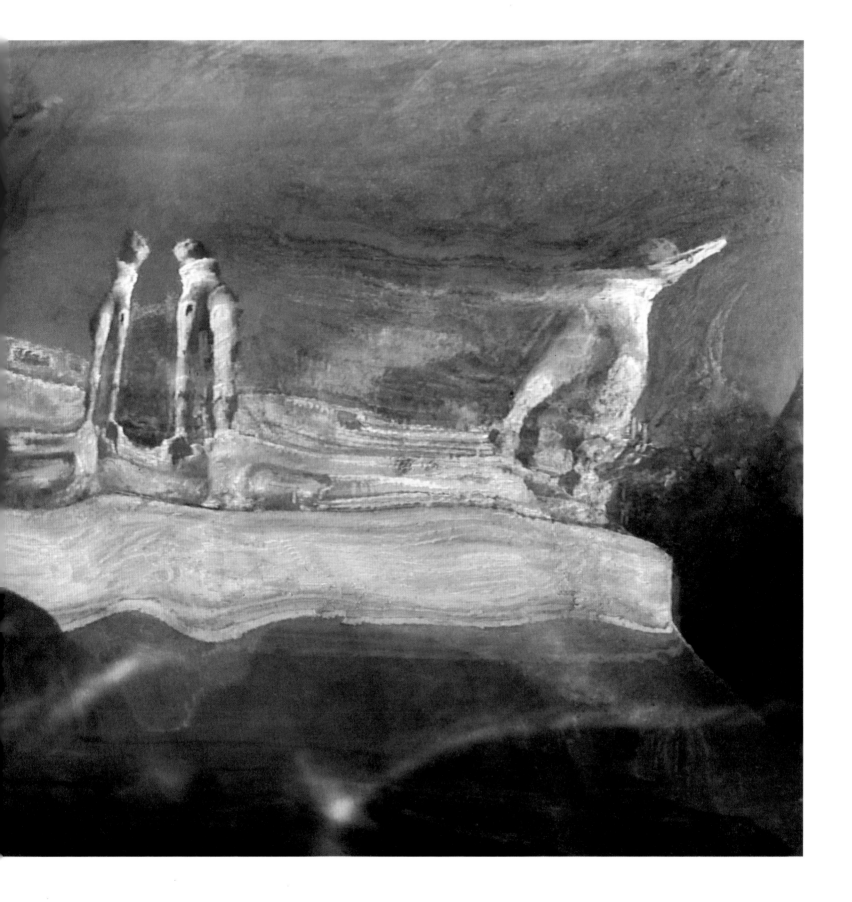

### THE LIE OF LOVE

But these are all lies. Men have died from time to time,
and worms have eaten them, but not for love.

—Rosalind, *As You Like It*, 4.1

### THE COUNTERFEITED BEAM

As plays the sun upon the glassy stream,
Twinkling another counterfeited beam,
So seems this gorgeous beauty to mine eyes.

—Suffolk, *1 Henry VI*, 5.5

### DREAMING ON BOTH

Thou hast nor youth nor age,
But as it were an after-dinner's sleep
Dreaming on both.

—Duke, *Measure for Measure*, 3.1

### GNAWING VULTURE OF THY MIND

I am Revenge, sent from th'infernal kingdom
To ease the gnawing vulture of thy mind
By working wreakful vengeance on thy foes.
Come down, and welcome me to this world's light.

—Tamora, *Titus Andronicus*, 5.2

## THIS BLESSED PLOT

This blessèd plot, this earth,
this realm, this England,
This nurse, this teeming womb
of royal kings.

—John of Gaunt, *Richard II*, 2.1

EXIT, PURSUED BY A BEAR

Exit, pursued by a bear.

—stage direction, *The Winter's Tale*, 3.3

JAQUES'S TRAVELS

It is a melancholy of mine own, compounded of many simples, extracted from many objects, and indeed the sundry contemplation of my travels.

—Jaques, *As You Like It*, 4.1

# EYED AWRY
## Rosamond Purcell

If you look at walls that are stained or made of different kinds of stones
and imagine some kind of scene, you begin to see in them certain picturesque views
of mountains, rivers, trees, plains, broad valleys, and hills of different shapes…
And all that appears confusedly on walls is very like the vibration of bells:
you can hear in their ringing all the sounds or words you want to imagine.

—LEONARDO

Last summer I found in a shop a mirrored but dingy mercury glass bottle fashionable among decorators. An early-twentieth-century apothecary jar, double-glazed and light-tight, it had originally held fabric dyes. For years I have photographed glass things, the objects they hold, and the shadows they cast: specimen bottles, Victorian glass plates, and windowpanes. I am drawn to the lenses in antique projectors, shadow on the wall of the cave reflections, and Cocteau's film *Orphée*, where the dead pass through mirrors as if through water.

Months earlier Michael Witmore had suggested a collaborative project inspired by Shakespeare; as the photographer, I was searching for a looking-glass way into the spirit of the age. This bottle gave me an idea and so, from another place down the road, I bought a few more. I took the empty vessels to a meadow in northern New Hampshire where I prayed that they would deliver up reflections worthy of Lear and Lady Macbeth. I turned them toward the light. Scarred by history and anamorphic in their reflecting properties, the bottles do not accommodate a single view without first changing it. Each is lined by two layers of close-set glass: the inner, a mirror, coated with silver in varying stages of rainbow oxidation, the outer grimy or gleaming.

From factory days negative impressions of long-gone buttons and tacks pressed against the glass impose themselves on the scene. In one dull mirrored surface the rib cage and jaws of a small fish appear and disappear—a fossil glimpsed and gone with the tide. And, as through water, when I began to work, the layers from inside cast unsteady shadows on the viewfinder and across the landscapes. Identification among reflected species grows uncertain as forms intermingle: animal becomes human; human, animal or vegetable—shades of Ovid's *Metamorphoses.* The wavering shapes begin to evoke the fluidity and multiple meanings found in speeches and verses of Shakespeare. Each element moves or dissolves if I shift the vantage point by so much as a millimeter. These come to be the shadows of this stage.

The scene may be framed by a curtain or scrim. I look in as through a peephole. Perhaps a miniature Elizabethan interior will appear. But the angle of view is always too wide and besides, not every aesthetic resolution occurs at the end of a tunnel.

Much of the action is played out downstage. Against the light, in the photo that eventually earned the title *Twenty Shadows* (page 38), each of the threadlike oxidized figures casts a shadow as though at a different time of day. As if on gallows and lost in the glare, they hover, souls above a dessicated ground. I show these mineral men to Mike, who all along by e-mail has been reading, rebuslike, the lines that occur to him as he sees the pictures day by day. He shoots back:

> Each substance of a grief hath twenty shadows
> Which shows like grief itself but is not so.
> For sorrow's eye, glazèd with blinding tears,
> Divides one thing entire to many objects—
> Like perspectives, which, rightly gazed upon,
> Show nothing but confusion; eyed awry,
> Distinguish form.
> —Bushy, *Richard II,* 2.2. 14–20

"'Perspectives,' for Shakespeare," he adds, "most likely represented anamorphic images." Of course! Bushy's last lines describe precisely how an anamorphic picture, stretched and

warped, shows "nothing but confusion" when viewed head-on. But, when eyed awry, that is, when viewed at an extreme angle to the plane of the image and so resolved, it will "distinguish form."

Unless representational models turn up (Ophelia, page 98) it is mighty hard, at any aperture, to get the Nikon to "distinguish form." It is a good thing that Mike knows where the words come from, for while I strive to evoke far-off yet familiar places like the forest of Ardenne, Lear's heath, or Elsinore I do not often remember what Shakespeare said about them. What I do hear, in the meadow, in lieu of sonnets or speeches, are sounds of mowing, of crows, of a distant dog, of thunder or, if lucky, the wind on the moor. Of course, any "real" atmosphere—clouds, blackflies, a blazing July and slow Indian summer—doesn't count. What counts must happen between the panes of glass, the transparent and the mirrored.

And all summer long, I know I am gambling, throwing the bones, casting the runes, sending up kite after kite in a storm.

The shapes of delicate trees, dendritic mineralizations embedded in the silvered layer of the bottles appear in the photographs. For centuries, fossils and minerals were taken to be biological mixtures of vegetable, animal, and stony substances. Human beings still attribute various meanings to images that appear in trees and stones. In Shakespeare's time, Nature, "a geometrician and optician, who uses all the laws of perspective, who is a painter,"[1] takes on the role of artist in the shaping of appearence.

In *Passing Strange* shapes have been exchanged, perverted, stolen. Human limbs grow arboreal, heads become stones, and the stones take to the sky. These tendencies match the drama and alchemy of the medium. Mercury is the substance once used to affix the silver to the glass. The Roman god Mercury was master of thieves. This glass is stealing from the landscape, consuming it and throwing back mere specters; counterfeit beam, a counterfeit bird (page 103).

Shakespeare uses mirrors to reflect the nature of twins or siblings, to show signs of moral corruption, beauty, self-loathing, and shame. And, like Montaigne, who writes that whatever is human is worthy of description, Shakespeare's characters speak as many feel, for when a loving connection dissolves, even now, time and again, it is "swift as a shadow, short as any dream, / Brief as the lightning in the collied night."[2] When one wonders what kind of creature one is anyway, Bottom from *Midsummer Night's Dream* comes to mind, the "rude mechanical" who, upon waking from having been translated into and back from

---

1. Jurgis Baltrusaitis, *Aberrations: An Essay on the Legend of Forms,* trans. by Richard Miller (Cambridge, Mass.: MIT Press, 1989), 73.
2. *A Midsummer Night's Dream* 1.1.144–45, spoken by Lysander; "collied" means coal-black.

being donkey-headed, says, "Methought I was—there is no man can tell what. Methought I was, and methought I had—."[3] At some point, about oneself, who has not felt to be—at least, a bit—of an ass?

Othello tells Desdemona tales of how he saw in a faroff land of deep caves and towering hills Anthropophagi and "men whose heads do grow beneath their shoulders."[4] She is a wonderful audience, her empathy for his travels and hard times like a mirror: "My story being done, / she gave me for my pains a world of sighs. / She swore in faith, 'twas strange, 'twas passing strange, / 'Twas pitiful, 'twas wondrous pitiful."[5]

In *Passing Strange* "Rumor" in the guise of female centaurs or Amazons appears; ghost warriors rise up and a shadow vulture looms. Castles, full-masted ships, St. Paul's, the church that burned down 350 years ago, rise and ebb, while across the plain, an uneasy huge-vined harvest spreads—part art, part reenactment, and, always, nature skewed.

Human pariahs emerge as insects, crabs, monsters, monkeys. In *Richard III*, the cripple and murderer climbs a bright spider, up inside a hollow tree, and, from *The Tempest*, Caliban, native but also outcast on his own island, appears as a water-breathing amphibian, gently communicating with a smaller version of himself. When in the play Trinculo, one of the shipwrecked party of the King of Naples, comes across the sleeping Caliban, he speculates, "What have we here, a man or a fish? Dead or alive?" He sniffs. "A fish, he smells like a fish; a very ancient and fish-like smell; a kind of not-of-the-newest poor-john."[6]

I have a long-standing affinity for hybrid beings and a fascination with natural conundrums but, over time, it is the language here that flashes and sings to me, in an inexplicable "Ah, I see it now—because what I hear is the song of what it must be…poor-john."

Working with the camera and the bottles is like recording stills from a time-lapse film. The camera is a free-form kaleidoscope. Chronology races and all becomes liquid and out of place. Time is like water, objects almost boneless, and whatever is fished out will not swim by again. All rules for previsualizing a photograph are without force when at play in this stream of the hybrids. I do not get "better" at working with the mercury bottles. From time to time, I do get lucky.

---

3. *A Midsummer Night's Dream* 4.1.202–3.
4. *Othello* 1.3.143–44. Anthropophagi are cannibals.
5. *Othello* 1.3.157–60; "sighs" at 158 (from Q) is an emendation of F "kisses."
6. *The Tempest*, 2.2.23–26; "poor-john" is dried hake.

# CONTEXTUAL NOTES

pages 2–3  THE UNDISCOVERED COUNTRY (Hamlet, *Hamlet*, 3.1.81)  In his famous "to be, or not to be" speech, Hamlet refers to death as "the undiscovered country," a "bourn" or boundary from which no traveler ever returns. The phrase captures Hamlet's dread at not knowing what comes after life, a dread he says leads us to rather "bear those ills we have / Than fly to others that we know not of" (3.1.83–84).

page 6  MADLY SHOT STARS (Oberon, *A Midsummer Night's Dream*, 2.1.149–54)  Oberon, King of Fairies, describes a scene he once saw while looking out over the ocean: a mermaid, riding on a dolphin's back, sang a tune so sweet or "dulcet" that the seas became calm and the stars—which usually move in perfect heavenly circles—jumped or "shot" from their "spheres" in admiration.

pages 12–13  THE MESSENGER APPROACHES (Dion, *The Winter's Tale*, 3.1.18–21)  In this harrowing tale of jealousy and redemption, Queen Hermione of Sicilia is accused of adultery by her husband Leontes, who suspects that their child is not his. He sends the messengers Dion and Cleomenes to consult the oracle of Apollo, where they are amazed to hear the oracle's "ear-deaf'ning voice." Here Dion tells his companion what they expect to learn once the judgment of the oracle is "discovered" or made known.

pages 14–15  FALSTAFF'S ESCAPE (Mistress Page, *The Merry Wives of Windsor*, 3.3.106–8)  Falstaff is trying to seduce two married women—Mistress Page and Mistress Ford—at the same time. Aware of his duplicity and looking for revenge, the women engineer a humiliating scene in which Falstaff must be secretly carried out in a basket of dirty laundry (bucking) to avoid being discovered by Mistress Ford's jealous husband. The scene takes place during "whiting time," when households send their laundry to a meadow near the Thames for cleaning by "whitsters" or bleachers. Unlike the smaller loads that will be hauled by housewives and servants on that day, the overburdened basket containing Falstaff will be carried by two men and dumped unceremoniously in a muddy ditch near the river.

pages 16–17  AN ART THAT NATURE MAKES (Polixenes, *The Winter's Tale*, 4.4.90–92)  Polixenes, the King of Bohemia, is engaged in a debate about flowers and grafting with Perdita at a sheep shearing feast. Perdita, unaware that she is a princess who was once abandoned by her father, who suspected she was illegitimate, argues that mixing different types of flowers—grafting—is a perversion of nature. Polixenes, in a witty phrase that summarizes an entire Renaissance philosophy of art, responds by saying that the art of grafting is rather "an art that nature makes." Nature thus can be enhanced by human craft, because the craft itself is natural.

pages 18–19  MALAPROP CONSTABLE (Dogberry, *Much Ado About Nothing*, 4.2.50–51)  Dogberry, a Constable in Messina, is an incompetent lawman who inadvertently manages to unravel a plot against Hero, the play's innocent heroine. Dogberry and his band create confusion wherever they go, in part because the Constable, like his sidekick Verges, has a habit of substituting words, such as "redemption" for "damnation," whenever he becomes excited—in this case, while Dogberry is berating a man captured by the watch.

page 20  RUDE MECHANICALS (Robin, *A Midsummer Night's Dream*, 3.2.8–11)  The mischievous Robin Goodfellow describes a plot he has laid for Titania, Queen of Fairies. He has applied a magical juice to her eyes while she lay sleeping; when awake, she will fall in love with the first person she sees. That person turns out to be one of the "mechanicals" or manual laborers gathered nearby to rehearse a play. Robin delights in what is about to happen: the Queen of Fairies is going to be enchanted by the lover she takes from this nearby crew of "patches" or fools.

page 21  THE BLASTED HEATH (Macbeth, *Macbeth*, 1.3.73–76)  Three witches approach Macbeth and Banquo on a blighted ("blasted") heath and address them in unfamiliar terms. Macbeth is hailed as Thane of Glamis—his current title, inherited from his father—but he is also addressed as Thane of Cawdor and future king. Wondering at this "prophetic greeting," Macbeth asks the bearded witches how they have obtained their predictions or "strange intelligence."

pages 22–23  AWAKE YOUR FAITH (Paulina, *The Winter's Tale*, 5.3.87–89)  The kingdom of Sicilia is in mourning. For many years Sicilia's king, Leontes, has been repenting the wrongs he'd done to his wife, Hermione, who seems to have died as a result of his false accusations of infidelity. In this scene, he and his daughter Perdita visit a statue of the queen that has been presented to them by Paulina, a longtime defender of the queen's honor. As father and daughter look at this remarkable figure, Paulina tells them to prepare to witness a transformation. You must "awake your faith," she says, and with a musical flourish she bids the long-dead queen come to life.

pages 24–25  THE OSTLER'S PLACE (First Carrier, *1 Henry IV*, 2.1.1–3)  Two carriers, men hired to transport goods, have risen before daybreak and entered the courtyard of the inn where they spent the night. Talking about their plans in the early morning hours, they complain that the inn breeds fleas and the service is terrible: they cannot get timely help with their horses from the "ostler" or horse attendant, even though "Charles's Wain" or the Big Dipper has already risen in the sky over the chimney.

page 26  PERDITA'S LANDING (Antigonus, *The Winter's Tale*, 3.3.48–50)  Antigonus is a loyal servant to King Leontes of Sicilia, the man who accused his innocent wife of adultery and demanded that her newborn child be abandoned as a bastard. Here Antigonus, who has taken the child to the shores of Bohemia, lays the child on the ground with a box and a scroll—tokens that will identify her as Leontes's long-lost heir. Also believing her mother guilty, Antigonus notes the portentous weather, exclaiming, "I never saw / The heavens so dim by day" (54–55).

page 27  OPEN YOUR EARS (Rumour, *2 Henry IV*, Induction, 1–2)  Shakespeare's second history play about Henry IV opens with a monologue by Rumour, a mythological figure who takes the stage in a robe "painted full of tongues." Rumour speaks with an irresistible voice: the "vent of hearing" or ear cannot be closed or "stopped" to what it has to say.

pages 28–29  REMEMBERING OLD ST. PAUL'S (Falstaff, *2 Henry IV*, 1.2.44–46)  Bardolph, the laconic serving man of Sir John Falstaff, was acquired by the dissolute knight at St. Paul's church, the cathedral at the center of London where servants sold their services. During Shakespeare's career as a playwright, St. Paul's was missing its tall steeple, which had been destroyed by lightning in 1561. Falstaff talks idly here about what can be had for money in London: he acquired his servant at Paul's, his servant is buying him a horse at the nearby market in Smithfield, and he might even be able to purchase a wife in the "stews" or whorehouses on the south bank of the Thames.

page 30  ALL ARE FLED (Edgar, *King Lear*, 3.6.26–28)  Lear has been spurned by his two older daughters and turned out of doors to wander the fields. He takes shelter outside of Gloucester's castle, where Gloucester's estranged son Edgar—himself disguised as a madman called "Poor Tom"—listens to Lear's complaints. Lear says that even the little dogs bark at him, which prompts Tom to make a boast: with a simple gesture of his head ("throwing thus"), he can make the dogs leap over a half-door, fleeing the old man's company.

page 31  LIE FURTHER OFF (Hermia, *A Midsummer Night's Dream*, 2.2.62–63)  Condemned by her father for choosing a man he doesn't approve of, Hermia flees with her lover Lysander into the woods of Athens. They plan to marry at Lysander's aunt's house seven leagues away but become lost while "wand'ring in the wood." Careful of her chastity, Hermia tells Lysander to find his own bed, but her lover protests his innocence in desiring to lie with her, "two bosoms and a single troth." He may "riddle...prettily," she says, but Hermia still wants him to sleep somewhere else.

pages 32–33  REMEMBER ME (Ghost, *Hamlet*, 1.5.61–64)  The ghost of Hamlet's dead father has drawn the prince away from the other men on the watch to tell a terrifying story. Old King Hamlet, enjoying what he thought was a "secure" sleep in his orchard, was killed by his brother Claudius. The murder is especially horrifying, for the poison ("hebanon") poured into the king's ear caused his skin instantly to become scaly as tree bark, a condition associated with leprosy.

pages 34–35  OTHELLO GREETS DESDEMONA IN CYPRUS (Othello, *Othello*, 2.1.178)  Othello, a Moor who fights for the Venetian republic against the Turks, has married Desdemona, daughter of a powerful Venetian senator. The marriage is bitterly opposed by her father, who cannot accept that his daughter would fall in love with an outsider. The Senate resolves the issue in the young couple's favor, sending Othello and his new wife on to Cyprus, where Othello is needed to fight the Turks. A storm wipes out the Turkish fleet, but Desdemona—having traveled to Cyprus on a separate ship—is anxious to see her husband. Safely arrived on land, Othello greets his new wife with a playful misnomer, calling her "fair warrior."

page 36–37 BORING THE MOON (Clown, *The Winter's Tale*, 3.3. 84–88) On the Bohemian shoreline, a "clown" or rustic peasant meets his father, the Old Shepherd, who has just found an abandoned child. The child is the daughter of King Leontes who, out of a jealous suspicion of her bastardy, ordered Antigonus to expose her. The Clown reports on the fortunes of the ship that brought Antigonus and the child (and the man who left her there) to Bohemia: all those aboard were lost in the frothing sea, whose tumult made the waters indistinguishable from the sky. Tossed on the waves, the Clown says that the ship appeared to be "boring" or piercing the moon itself.

page 38 TWENTY SHADOWS (Bushy, *Richard II*, 2.2.14–20) Bushy is a follower of King Richard II, who has just left for Ireland after having banished Harry Bolingbroke, the powerful Duke of Hereford. Bolingbroke's friends are enraged to see how King Richard enriches himself with the departed Duke's estate and they now plan a rebellion. Richard's wife, anxious about his departure for Ireland and fearing the worst, feels a strange, foreboding "grief." Bushy tries to calm her with an optical analogy: sorrow is causing her to look at the world from a distorting angle (eying it "awry") and to believe that she sees something real there—as in an anamorphic or stretched image—where there is instead only shadowy confusion.

page 39 THE RETURN TO ELSINORE (Hamlet, *Hamlet*, 4.6.13–16) After killing Polonius, Hamlet is sent to England where—according to his uncle's sealed orders—he will be killed instantly. Hamlet, however, intercepts these orders and rewrites them, sending the messengers themselves to their doom. By extraordinary coincidence, Hamlet's ship is met by pirates and, in the mêlée or "grapple," he manages to board their ship. The

pirates agree to return him to Denmark, where he can take revenge on his uncle.

pages 40–41 MIRANDA SEES THE STORM (Miranda, *The Tempest*, 1.2.1–6) Miranda has lived on an island since she was a young child with her father, Prospero, the exiled Duke of Milan and a magician. Prospero now has a chance to take revenge on his brother Antonio, who usurped Prospero's dukedome and is now passing by on a ship. Prospero arranges for a storm to waylay the ship but, seeing its terrible power, Miranda begs her father to take mercy on its passengers, tossed about as they are on a sea that rises to the sky's or "welkin's" cheek.

pages 42–43 CALIBAN'S FREEDOM (Caliban, *The Tempest*, 2.2.175–76) Caliban is a native of the island where Prospero and his daughter are living in exile. Born to the witch Sycorax and privy to the island's secrets, Caliban is forced into servitude by Prospero's magical powers of coercion. In this scene, Caliban encounters Stefano—a drunken butler newly arrived on the island from Milan—who plies him with drink. Giddy with a new sense of freedom, Caliban sings a song in which he declares his new allegiance to Stefano and tells his old master, Prospero, to "get a new man."

pages 44–45 TO ONE THING CONSTANT Never (Balthasar, *Much Ado About Nothing*, 2.3.56–59) Balthasar, a singer in the court of the Aragonese prince Don Pedro, is invited to sing a love song (with string-instrument accompaniment) for Don Pedro and his friends. The words of the song warn women about the inconstancy of men's affection—always halfway between sea and shore. Benedick, listening nearby and skeptical of love, wonders how an instrument made of "sheep's guts" can rouse men's spirits. Benedick will soon be tricked into an affair of his own with Beatrice, his equal in wariness and volubility.

page 46 GREY-EYED MORN (Friar Laurence, *Romeo and Juliet*, 2.2.1–4) Romeo, an impulsive but eloquent young man, enlists the aid of his confessor Friar Laurence to help him marry his new lover, Juliet. Before Romeo arrives on the scene, Friar Laurence—who concocts the sleeping potion that inadvertently dooms the couple—appears here gathering flowers and offering an epic description of the morning as it breaks through the night, forcing darkness to reel out of the pathway of the "fiery wheels" of the sun.

page 47 FERDINAND HEARS ARIEL'S SONG (Ferdinand, *The Tempest*, 1.2.391, 410-11) Ferdinand, the son of Alonso, King of Naples, has arrived on Prospero's island after being shipwrecked in a storm that he believes killed his father. Ariel, a spirit of the island, arrives to sing a song about this supposedly drowned king who lies "full fathom five," his bones made of "coral" and his eyes of "pearl." Ferdinand, who cannot locate the source of the music, believes that it must not be human or "mortal."

pages 48–49 DESCANT ON MY DEFORMITY (Richard, Duke of Gloucester, *Richard III*, 1.1.18–21) The fortunes of Richard of Gloucester and his family—the descendants of the house of York—have just begun to flower. Edward IV is now king of England, but his brother Richard cannot enjoy this happy turn of events. In the opening scene of the play, Richard describes how, born misshapen, he takes no pleasure in court life. His only consolation for his misfortune will be to seize the crown for himself. Otherwise all he can do is study his shadow on the ground and curse ("descant upon") his deformity.

pages 50–51 AUMERLE SPEEDS TO THE KING (Duchess of York, *Richard II*, 5.2.111–13, 117) King Richard II has been displaced by Harry Bolingbroke, now Henry IV. Aumerle's father, the Duke of York—once loyal to the old king and now to Henry—discovers that his son, Aumerle, is part of a plot to kill the new king. As York departs for the court to inform on his own son, his wife (the Duchess of York) urges Aumerle to take action: ride to the king, she says, and beg forgiveness before your father arrives to accuse you!

pages 52–53 BARREN WINTER (Duke Humphrey of Gloucester, *2 Henry VI*, 2.4.1–4) Duke Humphrey has acted as Lord Protector under Henry VI, but the king has now assumed full responsibilities for his reign. This transition occurs at a low point for Humphrey: his wife, Dame Eleanor Cobham, was caught associating with a witch and has been sentenced to walk the streets barefoot in a white sheet. Humphrey believes this punishment is just. Before she appears barefoot on stage, he speaks these lines, acknowledging stoically that winter or bad fortune "evermore succeeds" or follows the good times of summer.

pages 54–55 THE WARS TO COME (Bishop of Carlisle, *Richard II*, 4.1.131–35) Harry Bolingbroke, in a position to take the English throne by force, has just learned that King Richard II has decided to descend the throne and turn the scepter over to him. The Bishop of Carlisle, a long-standing supporter of Richard, prophesies that nothing good will come of the extra-lineal accession of Bolingbroke. Because it occurs under duress, this abrupt shift in allegiances will create strife among families (confounding "kin with kin"), plaguing the country with civil war.

pages 56–57 MASSACRE (King Harry, *Henry V*, 4.6.35–38) Significantly outnumbered at the Battle of Agincourt, Henry V's soldiers nevertheless manage to seize the advantage on the battlefield. In this scene, Henry listens to a moving story about the death of two English nobles in battle. Then, sensing commotion but unaware that his troops have prevailed, Henry believes that the French are regrouping for another attack. He commands that the prisoners already taken from the French be killed immediately, a bloodthirsty act, even in wartime.

pages 58–59 FEEDING ON ENGLAND (Captain, *2 Henry VI*, 4.1.83–85) After having enjoyed remarkable power at court, the Duke of Suffolk is now on the run, banished by King Henry VI. Suffolk, who operated as a go-between during Henry's courtship of Princess Margaret in France and was for a time her lover, worked as a force behind the throne during the king's minority. Here, Suffolk, banished by King Henry and fleeing the country, has been apprehended by a sea captain on his way to France. Before Suffolk is killed by the master's mate, the captain condemns Suffolk's ambition and stratagems ("policy") at court: like the mythological beast Sylla (or Scylla), he says to Suffolk, you have gorged yourself on the flesh of your country.

pages 60–61 THE FIELD OF CLOTH OF GOLD (Norfolk, *All Is True (Henry VIII)*, 1.1.18–21) The Duke of Norfolk introduces this play about the intrigues of Henry VIII's court by giving an eyewitness account of the meeting between the French king Francis I and Henry VIII of England near Calais in June of 1520. This now famous historical event, noted for its displays of wealth and pageantry, became known as "The Field of Cloth of Gold." Norfolk's remarks call attention to the competitive nature of the festivities he sees in Calais as each monarch attempts to outdo the other by surrounding himself in "clinquant"—or glittering—surroundings.

page 62  IN SPRINGTIME (Pages, *As You Like It*, 5.3.32–35)  Touchstone, a clown from the French court, has retired with two ladies to the Forest of Ardenne, where he has met and wooed a goatherd named Audrey. In this scene, the betrothed couple is treated to a lighthearted pastoral song celebrating the "seize-the-moment" spirit of youth and springtime.

page 63  KISSING-COMFITS (Falstaff, *The Merry Wives of Windsor*, 5.5.16–18)  Sir John Falstaff is in for a final humiliation from Mistresses Page and Ford, the two women he has been trying to seduce simultaneously in this farcical drama of erotic intrigue. Falstaff has been told to meet Mistress Ford at Herne's Oak in the park at midnight; instead of a tryst, however, he will be treated to a fright at the hands of a troupe of "fairies" (children in disguise). Dressed in an absurd deer outfit, Falstaff cries out jubilantly to his "doe" in the night, calling down prodigious weather events that will complement his erotic exploits—a rain of potatoes, of candies or "comfits," and of aphrodisiac oysters or "eringoes."

pages 64–65  AN EMPTY SET (Jaques, *As You Like It*, 2.7.138–39)  An inveterate melancholic, Jaques is a favorite of the banished Duke Senior who lives in the woods with other members of his court. Jaques, who can "suck melancholy out of a song as a weasel sucks eggs" (2.5.11–12), is here reflecting on the roles people play in the pageant of life, moving as they do from infancy through adulthood and thence to the "second childhood" of old age. Knowing the script or qualities assigned to each of these ages and roles, Jaques views this drama with a resigned amusement, one that shades at times into contempt.

page 66  THE COWARDLY EARTH (Glendower, *1 Henry IV*, 3.1.12–16)  In this scene Owain Glyndŵr, a Welsh rebel feared and detested by Henry IV, meets with Hotspur, a high-spirited nobleman from Northumberland, to plot against the king. Glyndŵr remarks that the king wishes Hotspur were in heaven, so troublesome is he to his reign. When Hotspur says that the king has similar feelings toward Glyndŵr, Glyndŵr—boasting of the prodigious events that accompanied his birth or "nativity"—claims the "front" or forehead of heaven was filled with fiery "cressets" (metal baskets of fire) and the earth quaked in fear.

page 67  YOUTH IN WINTER (Katherine, *The Taming of the Shrew*, 4.6.46–48)  In this scene, the once shrewish Katherine is instructed by her husband, Petruccio, to greet an old man they have met on the road as if he were a "gentle mistress." Obliging, Kate calls him a "budding virgin," whereupon Petruccio demands that she address him as the old man that he is. Kate pivots effortlessly, saying that the sun has made her see everything as if it were green, mistaking an older man—one in the winter of life—for springtime's virgin.

pages 68–69  DEAF AND DULL (Aaron, *Titus Andronicus*, 2.1.129–32)  Aaron the Moor is plotting against Titus Andronicus, a powerful Roman general. Aaron urges Chiron and Demetrius to rape Titus's daughter, Lavinia, when she goes into the woods to hunt. Aaron goads them with thoughts of their advantage, pointing out that the woods have no eyes and ears: the brutal acts they commit will be witnessed by no one, as they will be "shadowed from heaven's eye."

pages 70–71  THE CONJURER, PROSPERO (Prospero, *The Tempest*, 1.2.188–89)  In this scene, Prospero has just called for his spirit Ariel—a "puck" or mischievous spirit—who does the magician's bidding around the island where they live. Ariel tells Prospero that he has created a tempest in order to waylay a passing ship, having "flamed amazement...on the top-mast, the yards, and the bowsprit." This scene gives us our first glimpse of Prospero's powers, powers he will use at first to dazzle and to torment his enemies but which eventually he must renounce to avoid being corrupted by his own desire for revenge.

pages 72–73  A DUCHESS'S CURSE (Duchess of York, *Richard III*, 4.4.26–30)  In the course of a brutal dynastic struggle that has pitted families and generations against one another, Richard III has become king. Here three widows gather to curse the bloodshed that has accompanied his ascent to the throne. The Duchess of York, whose sons and grandchildren have fallen to Richard's ambitions, curses the course of English history with prophetic intensity: like a revenant, or living corpse, the crimes of England's rulers will return to stalk the "lawful earth."

pages 74–75  BARE FORKED ANIMAL (Lear, *King Lear*, 3.4.95–97)  Lear is huddled in the rainy fields with his fool Kent and the grimy madman "Poor Tom." Kent is a banished nobleman who has returned to serve Lear; "Poor Tom" is really Edgar, loyal son of Gloucester, who has been forced by slander to flee his home. Lear senses something profound in Tom's

abject poverty: Tom, he feels, displays humanity in its natural, "unaccommodated" state. Reduced to living like a beast—like a two-legged or "forked" animal—Tom shows Lear a kind of suffering that mocks all kingly pretensions to civility.

pages 76–77 THE PREPARATION OF OPHELIA (First Clown, *Hamlet*, 5.1.1–2) Two "clowns" or peasants are digging a grave for Ophelia, whose death appears to have been by suicide (a sin). The coroner has conducted an inquest and, perhaps because of her connections at court, Ophelia will be buried in consecrated ground. The first gravedigger has substituted the word "salvation" for "damnation" in his question, but the sense of the question remains: does Ophelia deserve to be buried here?

pages 78–79 DREAMERS OFTEN LIE (Romeo, *Romeo and Juliet*, 1.4.49) Romeo and Mercutio, dressed in aristocratic dancing or "masquing" costumes, prepare to enter the costumed "feast" at the house of the Capulets, enemies of Romeo's family. Romeo is reluctant to enter the house—whether out of melancholy or for fear of the Capulets, it is not clear. He is urged on by Mercutio, who is most anxious to join in the festivities. When asked why he feels it is unwise to enter, Romeo explains his hesitations cryptically, saying, "I dreamt a dream tonight."

pages 80–81 THE SWELLING SCENE (Chorus, *Henry V*, Prologue, 1–4) In keeping with a common Renaissance stage convention, a Chorus or speaking Prologue arrives on stage to announce the play that is about to be performed. In this case, the Chorus describes the poet's task in epic terms: he asks for a muse of fire to inspire the playwright's creative faculty or "invention." Through the miracle of drama, a simple wooden stage becomes host to an expansive or "swelling" scene of monarchs, kingdoms, and, later, entire armies.

page 82 THE PENALTY (Shylock, *The Merchant of Venice*, 4.1.98–99) Shylock, although derided as a Jew in Venice, nevertheless agrees to provide a loan to the Christian merchant Antonio in exchange for an unusual surety: if Antonio is unable to pay back the interest-free loan, he will—"in a merry sport"—agree to forfeit an "equal" or exact pound of flesh. The "merry" condition becomes deadly serious when Shylock's daughter elopes, taking a store of treasures with her. When he hears that Antonio will not be able to repay the loan, Shylock turns his attention away from his own losses to consider those he might

inflict on others. He will now demand the bloody penalty for forfeit of his bond.

page 83 'TIS THE EYE OF CHILDHOOD (Lady Macbeth, *Macbeth*, 2.2.51–53) Just as Macbeth and his wife have planned, he has murdered the king who came as a guest to his castle. Terrified at the murder he has just committed, Macbeth brings the bloody weapons to his wife and refuses to return them to the scene for fear of "thinking" on what he has done. Lady Macbeth mocks his paralysis, saying that the dead man (or his sleeping guards) can do no harm: only a child is afraid of pictures.

pages 84–85 UNBURIED (Titus, *Titus Andronicus*, 1.1.86–88) Titus has just returned from a military campaign in which he subdued the Goths and brought back as prisoners their queen and several of her sons. In this scene, Titus draws attention to his own dead sons whom he has brought back to Rome to be interred with their ancestors. As long as they remain unburied, they cannot cross the river Styx to the underworld and Titus will have failed to do justice to his kin or "kind."

pages 86–87 THE BOOK, THE LAND (Soothsayer, *Antony and Cleopatra*, 1.2.8–9) In this amusing scene, Cleopatra's serving women ask a soothsayer to inspect their palms and tell them their fortunes. Charmian, who hopes to "be married to three kings in a forenoon and widow them all," asks the soothsayer if he "knows things," to which the latter modestly replies that he can read "a little" of nature's infinite book of secrets.

pages 88–89 SUBTLE AS SPHINX (Biron, *Love's Labour's Lost*, 4.3.316–19) Biron is one of several courtiers who have sworn an oath to avoid the company of women for three years in the pursuit of scholarship and knowledge. He and his colleagues fail miserably in their plan. In this speech, Biron wittily—but also somewhat glibly—explains that love is the greatest tutor of them all. Possessing the virtues of subtlety and harmony, love can charm the heavens with its voice, inducing the gods to join in with a sleep-inducing harmony.

page 90 THIS QUEEN WILL LIVE (Cerimon, *Pericles*, 12.90–93) Cerimon, a physician in Ephesus, is witness to a marvel: a coffin containing the body of a woman who died in childbirth has washed ashore with a note from her royal husband, Pericles, asking the finder to give his wife a proper burial. Cerimon is

convinced that the queen can be revived. Striking up music, he gives her a mysterious medicine. She has only been unconscious or "entranced" for five hours, he says, and within minutes she will be alive once more.

page 91 LET HELEN GO (Cassandra, *Troilus and Cressida*, 2.2.110–11) Paris of Troy seduced Helen and brought her home to Troy; they are now besieged by Greeks fighting for her return. Cassandra, a prophetess, has terrible news for her fellow Trojans assembled to discuss the siege: if they do not let Helen go, Troy will burn.

pages 92–93 HEAVEN's VAULT (Lear, *King Lear*, 5.3.2.31–34) Cordelia, the third and once spurned daughter of King Lear, has returned to Britain from exile and recovered her father, who was wandering in the fields. After a brief reunion in which Lear and Cordelia dream about a life together removed from courtly conflict, the traitor Edmond, imprisoning Cordelia, arranges to have her killed by her jailer. Edmond's treacheries are soon discovered and the order to murder Cordelia countermanded. But now Lear appears with a terrible revelation: the countermand arrived too late. Cordelia, whom he carries now in his arms, is "dead as earth," never to breathe again.

pages 94–95 WE ARE PICTURES (Claudius, *Hamlet*, 4.5.80–82) Spurned by Hamlet and stricken with grief at the death of her father, Ophelia has become unmoored. After a wrenching performance in which she sings distractedly on the lute and offers up bawdy riddles to Claudius and Gertude, the king declares that she has been "divided from herself." Without her former "fair judgement," she is a mere "picture" or animal—a likeness of life that lacks understanding.

pages 96–97 PETRUCCIO's HORSE (Biondello, *The Taming of the Shrew*, 3.2.48–52) Petruccio has a plan for "taming" Kate, the woman whom all of Padua refers to as a "shrew." After arranging with Kate's father to marry her, Petruccio barely arrives in time for their wedding ceremony. In a move calculated to humiliate her, he rides in on a horse that is literally on its last legs: it has air-restricting tumors ("windgalls"), swelled leg joints ("spavins"), jaundice ("yellows"), swollen glands ("fives"), the staggers, intestinal worms ("bots"), a crooked back, sprained shoulders, knock-knees ("near-legged"), and an improperly fitted or "half-cheeked" bit.

page 98 TILL THAT HER GARMENTS (Gertrude, *Hamlet*, 4.7.152–54) No one knows exactly how Ophelia died after her father was murdered and she was spurned by Hamlet. The closest we come, aside from hearing a debate between the two gravediggers about Ophelia's possible suicide, is a short, elegiac description delivered by Gertrude. Blaming the young woman's fall into the river on an "envious sliver" or twig that broke under her weight, Gertrude describes Ophelia singing abstractedly ("incapable of her own distress") as the water pulls her clothes and song (the "melodious lay") to muddy death.

page 99 THE SOUNDS AT DOVER CLIFFS (Gloucester, *King Lear*, 4.1.67–69) Literally blind, Gloucester realizes that he has also been blind in a more figurative sense to his bastard son's plot to defame Edgar, Gloucester's legitimate son. Giving up hope of ever seeing Edgar again, Gloucester is unaware that Edgar himself—now disguised as "Poor Tom"—has just joined him on his journey. Gloucester, who wants to commit suicide at the Dover Cliffs, asks Edgar to lead him there. Later Edgar fools him into believing that he has arrived at the cliffs when they are really standing in a field near Dover. Although the old man cannot hear the sound of the sea, he nevertheless believes he is on a precipice as he prepares to leap to his death.

pages 100–101 KNOW MY STOPS (Hamlet, *Hamlet*, 3.2.335–36) Claudius has sent for Hamlet's school friends Rosencrantz and Guildenstern to spy on his nephew. It takes only a moment for Hamlet to realize that his friends have not chosen to pay a spontaneous visit, but are in his uncle's service. Mocking them, Hamlet asks Guildenstern repeatedly if he will play a pipe that has been handed to him. When Guildenstern protests that he doesn't know the fingering, Hamlet instantly turns the tables to ask why, then, do you think you can play me?

page 102 THE LIE OF LOVE (Rosalind, *As You Like It*, 4.1.91–92) Orlando, not realizing that he is addressing his lover, Rosalind (in disguise), declares that he will die if she will not have him. Mocking this melodramatic view, Rosalind informs him that over the course of thousands of years, no man has died "in a love-cause." Men do indeed die, Rosalind says, "but not for love."

page 103 THE COUNTERFEITED BEAM (Suffolk, *1 Henry VI*, 5.5.18–20) The Earl of Suffolk has just met Margaret, daughter

of the King of Naples, who will eventually marry Henry VI through Suffolk's negotiations. Though daunted by her charms, Suffolk is immediately attracted to the princess. His eyes reflect her beauty, he says, like the glassy stream reflects or "counterfeits" the image of the sun.

pages 104–5 DREAMING ON BOTH (Duke, *Measure for Measure*, 3.1.32–34) Duke Vincentio has left his dukedom in Vienna in order to return in disguise: he wants to see how the city is governed in his absence. In this scene, he advises Claudio to accept the death sentence meted out to him by the Duke's ruling deputy. The Duke gives a number of well-worn Renaissance arguments designed to eliminate fear of death: life itself is not to be prized, as it is an after-dinner sleep in which we dream of the advantages of youth and age but have neither.

pages 106–7 GNAWING VULTURE OF THY MIND (Tamora, *Titus Andronicus*, 5.2.30–33) Tamora, Queen of the Goths and new wife of the Emperor Saturninus, arranges a false pageant in order to play on the fears of her enemy Titus Andronicus. Disguising herself as Revenge and her two sons as Rape and Murder, she offers to help Titus ease the "gnawing vulture" of his mind.

pages 108–9 THIS BLESSED PLOT (John of Gaunt, *Richard II*, 2.1.50–51) On his deathbed John of Gaunt—father of the future Lancastrian line of kings that will begin with Henry IV— prophesies that Richard will be brought low by the deceptive courtiers who have encouraged him to leave England to wage war in Ireland. "Violent fires soon burn out themselves," Gaunt says, and goes on to mourn the self-inflicted collapse of England, personified as nurse and womb of royal kings.

pages 110–11 EXIT, PURSUED BY A BEAR (stage direction, *The Winter's Tale*, 3.3.57) This notoriously improbable Shakespearean stage direction marks the moment when—after abandoning the infant princess on the Bohemian shore—the lord Antigonus is chased unceremoniously off stage, "pursued by a bear."

pages 112–13 JAQUES'S TRAVELS (Jaques, *As You Like It*, 4.1.14–16) Jaques is conversing with Rosalind and Celia, both traveling in disguise through the Forest of Ardenne. He announces that he loves melancholy "better than laughing," a disposition that Rosalind is quick to mock. Jaques nevertheless praises all of the different kinds of melancholy—that of the scholar, the musician, the courtier, the soldier, the lawyer, the lady, and the lover—concluding that his own melancholy is unique, mixed or "compounded" of many elements or "simples." These elements have been extracted from various sights or "objects" that Jaques has encountered in his travels (or, punningly, "travails"). His melancholy is thus as much a product of art as it is of experience.

page 127 MEADOW-FAIRIES (Mistress Quickly, *The Merry Wives of Windsor*, 5.5.62–63) Playing a part in the scheme to humiliate Sir John Falstaff, Mistress Quickly enters the Windsor Woods dressed as the Fairy Queen. Accompanied by a troupe of fairies (disguised children), she charges them to dance nightly in the circular shape or "compass" of a garter—the latter a famous chivalric symbol. During the revelry, Sir John is discovered cowering in the grass and taunted mercilessly by the fairies with pinches and burning candles.

page 128 TO FLY THE BOAR (Lord Hastings, *Richard III*, 3.2.25–27) Lord Stanley has just sent a messenger in the middle of the night to Lord Hastings: tonight he dreamed that a boar (the heraldic symbol of Richard of Gloucester) had razed his helmet. Stanley wants Hastings to flee with him to the north, but Hastings—unwisely, as it turns out—refuses to go, quoting a proverb to the effect that flight encourages the boar to strike when it would otherwise remain still.

MEADOW-FAIRIES

And nightly, meadow-fairies, look you sing,
Like to the Garter's compass, in a ring.

—Mistress Quickly, *The Merry Wives of Windsor*, 5.5

# ACKNOWLEDGMENTS

Rosamond Purcell thanks John Norton, Nina Williams, Richard Balzer, Katy Park, Julia Sheehan, Andrew McClellan, Wendy Watson, Liz and Steve Jackson, Libby's Bistro, and Andrew, John Henry, and Dennis Purcell.

Michael Witmore thanks Jim and Peggy Knapp, Dan Selcer, Theresa Smith, Rebecca Maatta, Marcy Norton, David Loewenstein, Gordon McMullan, and Kellie Robertson (sine qua non).

Michael Witmore and Rosamond Purcell express gratitude to Jill Casid, Linda Benedict-Jones, Erik Castillo, Steve Ennis, Gail Kern Paster, the staff at the Folger Shakespeare Library, Laura Lindgren, Jim Mairs, Austin O'Driscoll, Julia Reidhead, Giorgianna Ziegler, and the editors of the *Norton Shakespeare*.

TO FLY THE BOAR

To fly the boar before the boar pursues
Were to incense the boar to follow us,
And make pursuit where he did mean no chase.

—Lord Hastings, *Richard III*, 3.2